Is Nan In?

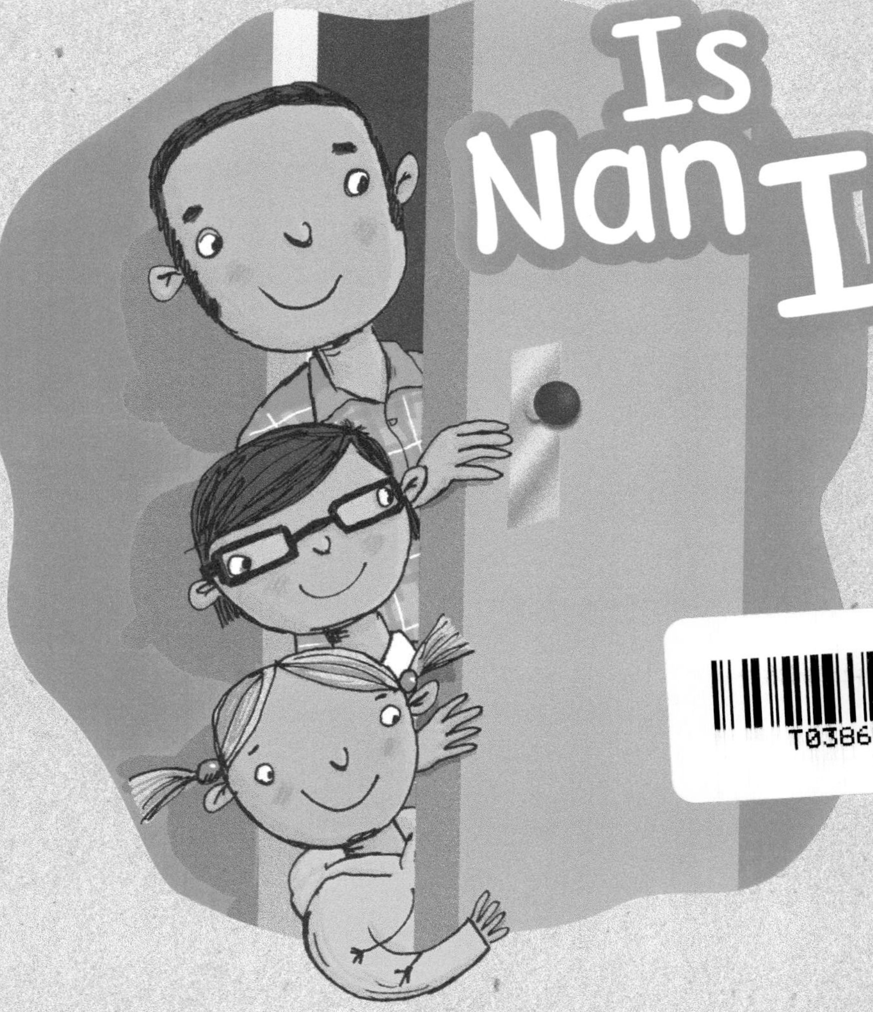

Written by Celia Warren
Illustrated by Andy Rowland

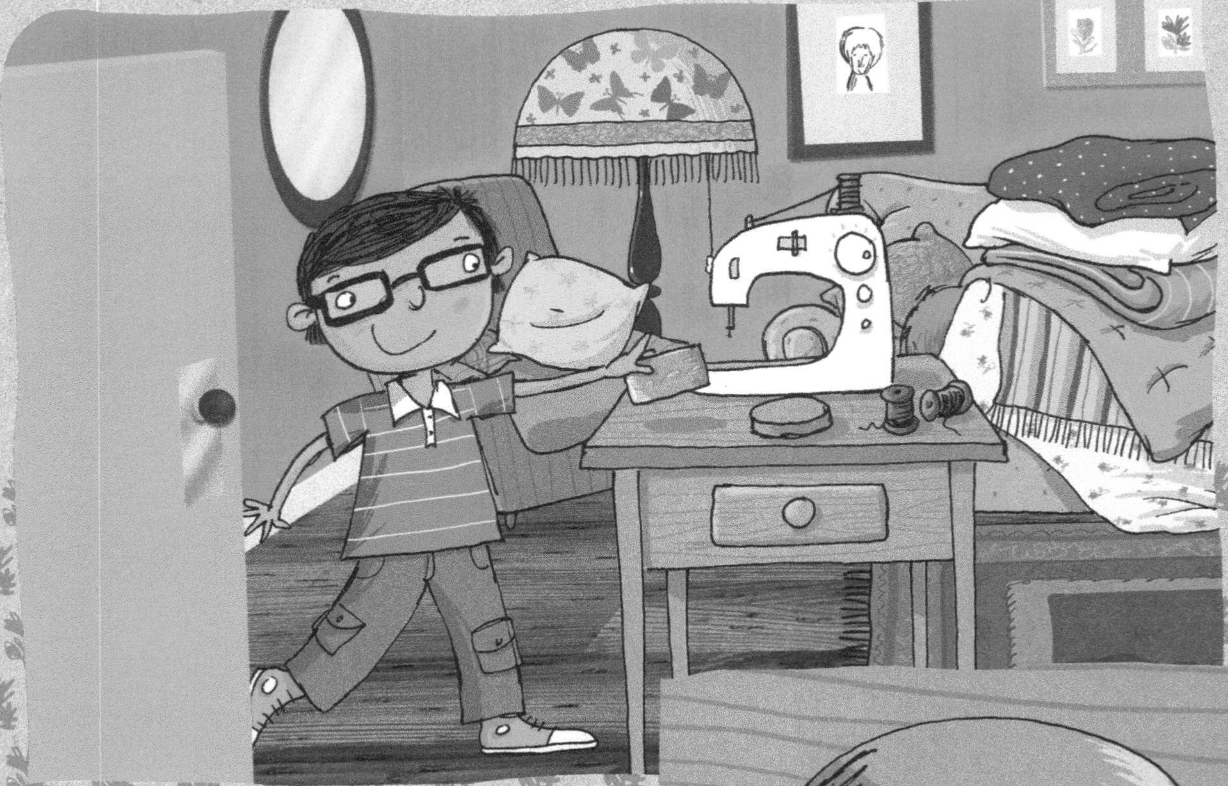

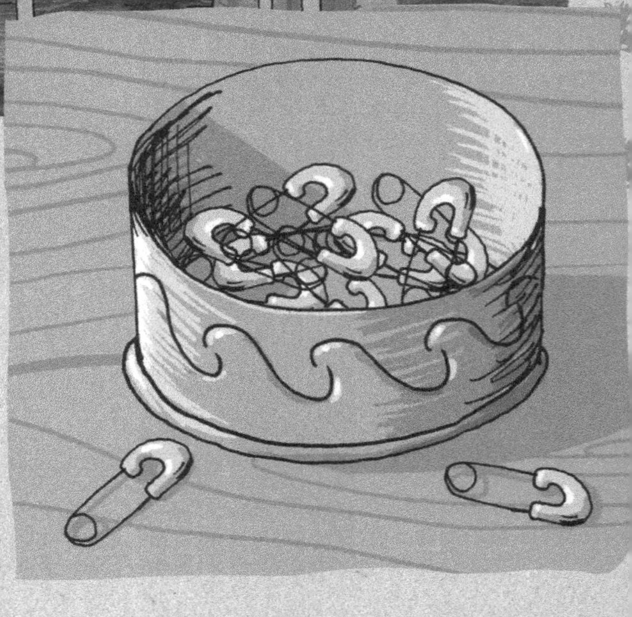

Nan's pins
sit in a tin.

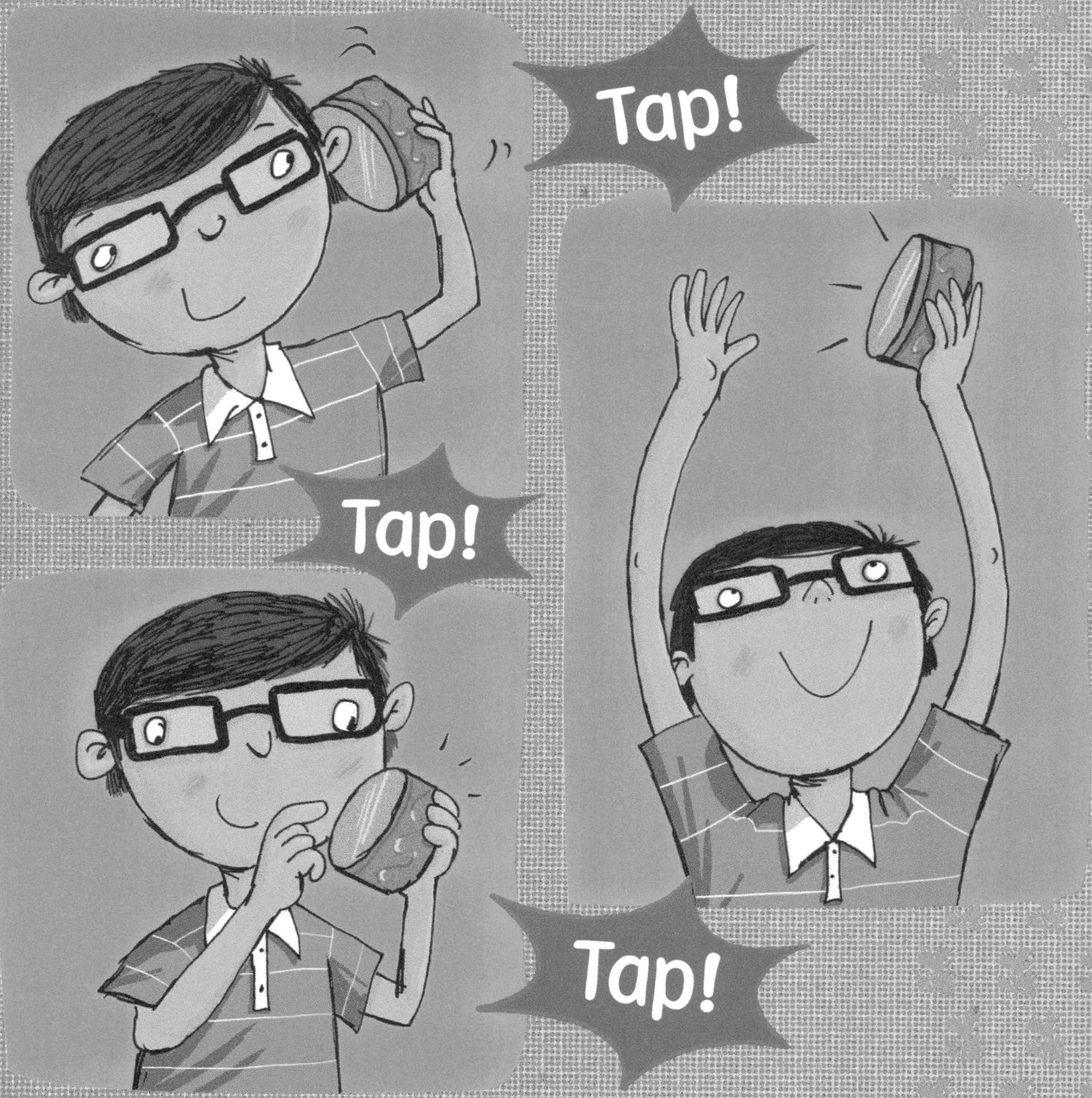
Tap!
Tap!
Tap!

Pam nips in.

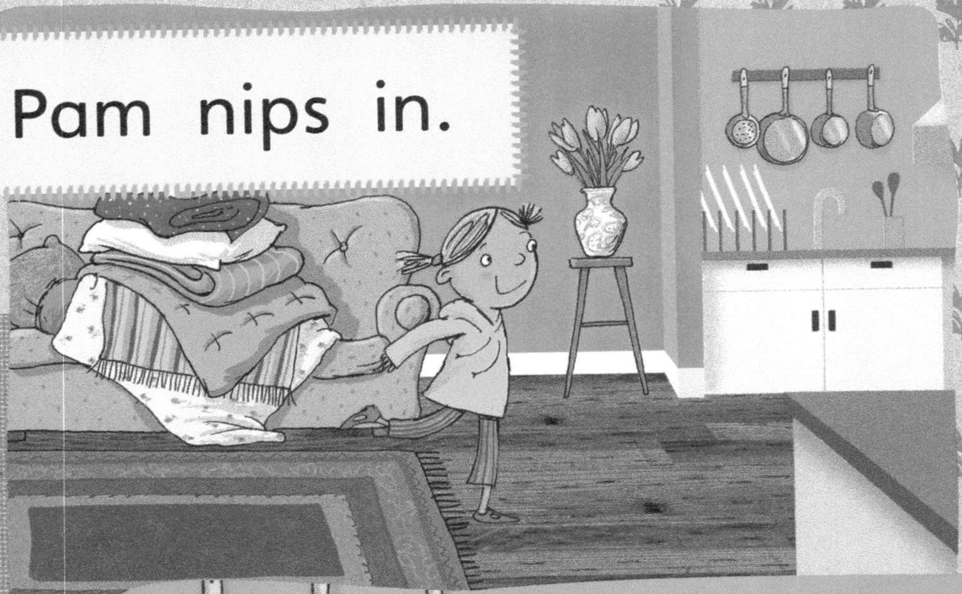

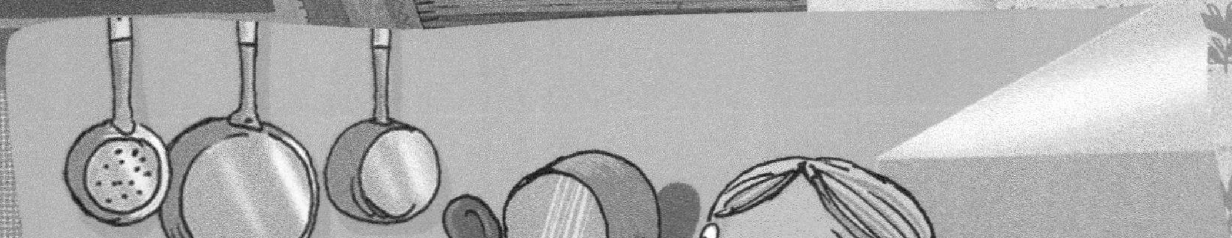

Pam taps pans.

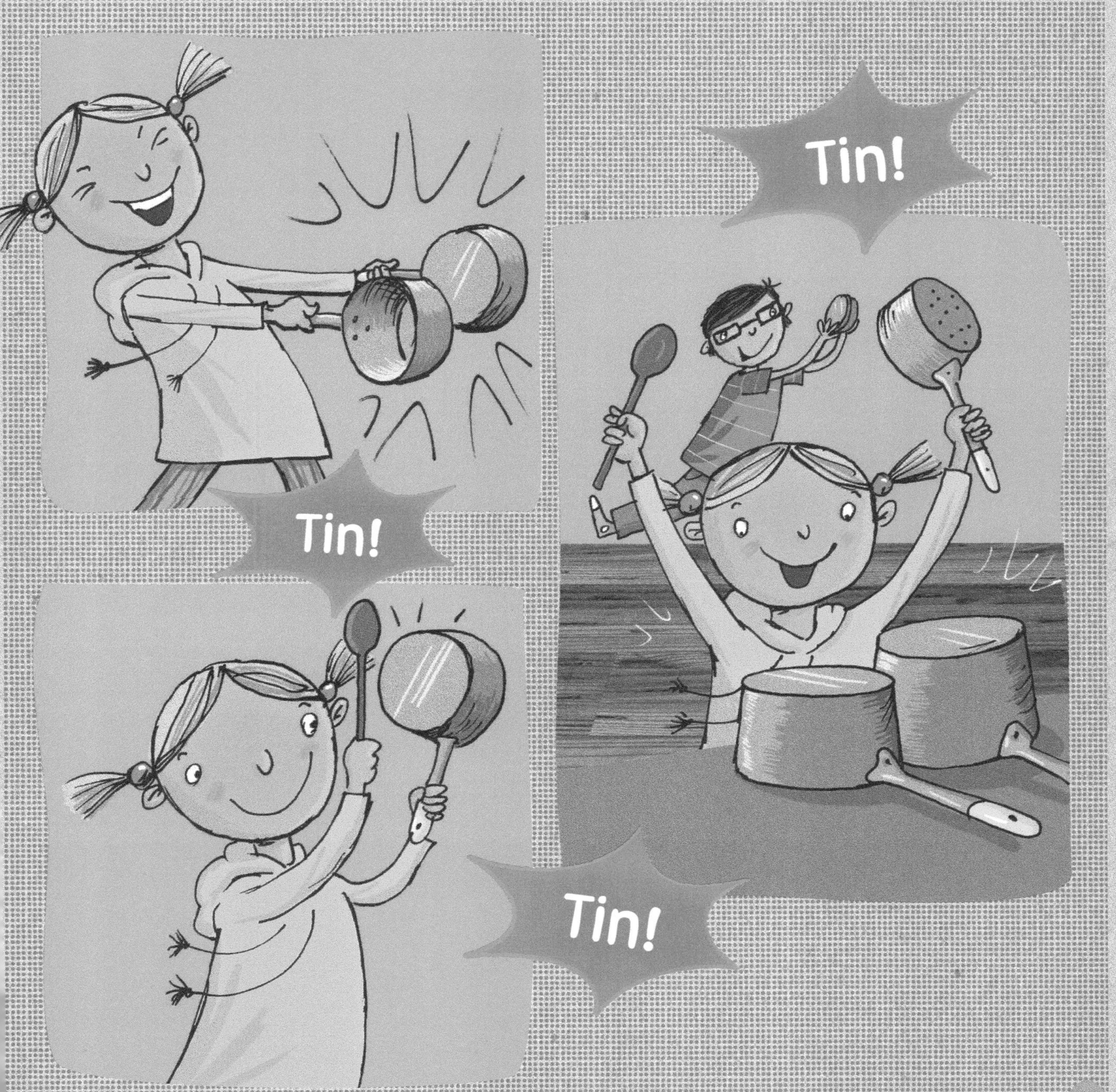
Tin!
Tin!
Tin!

Dad nips in.

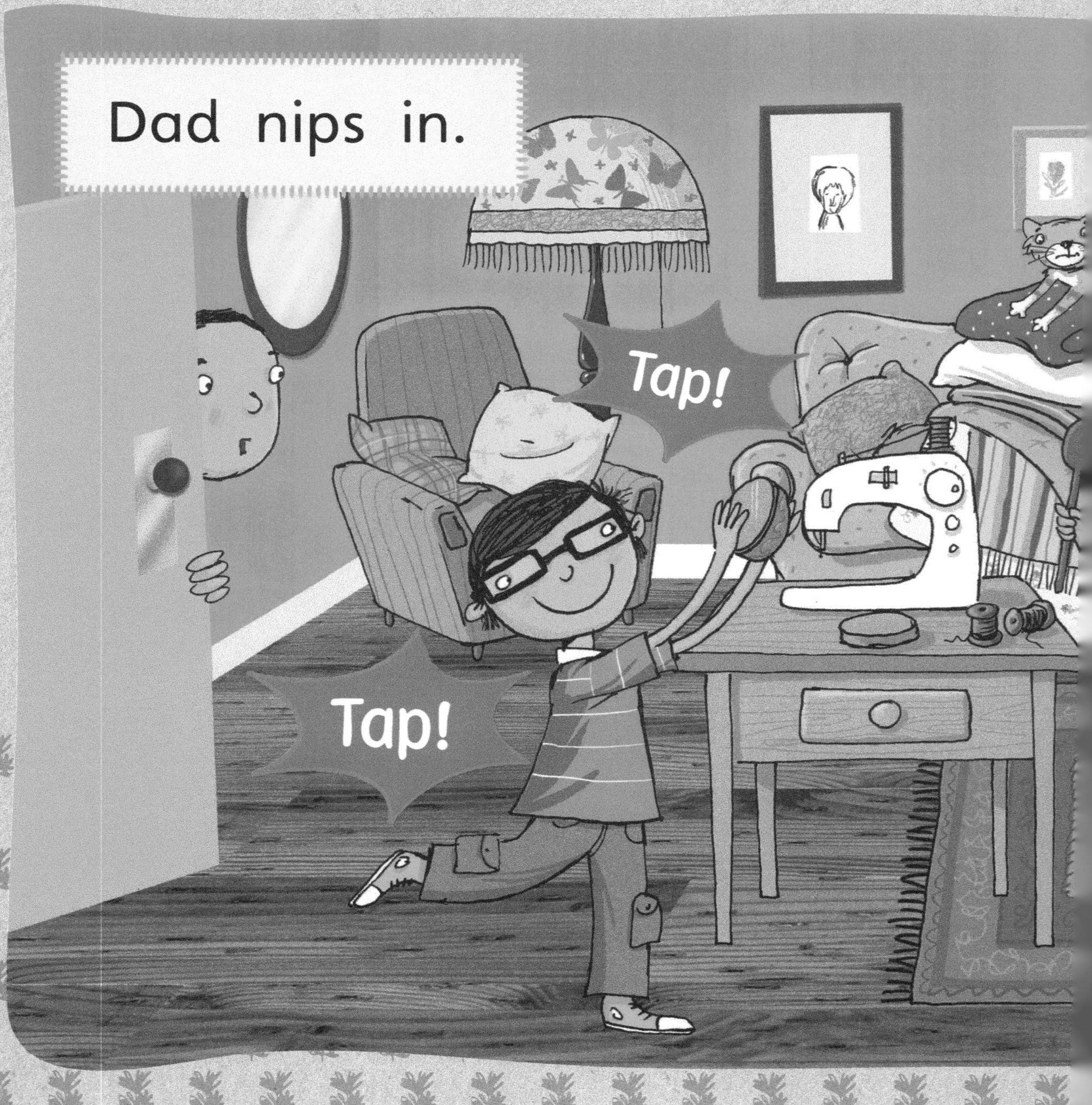

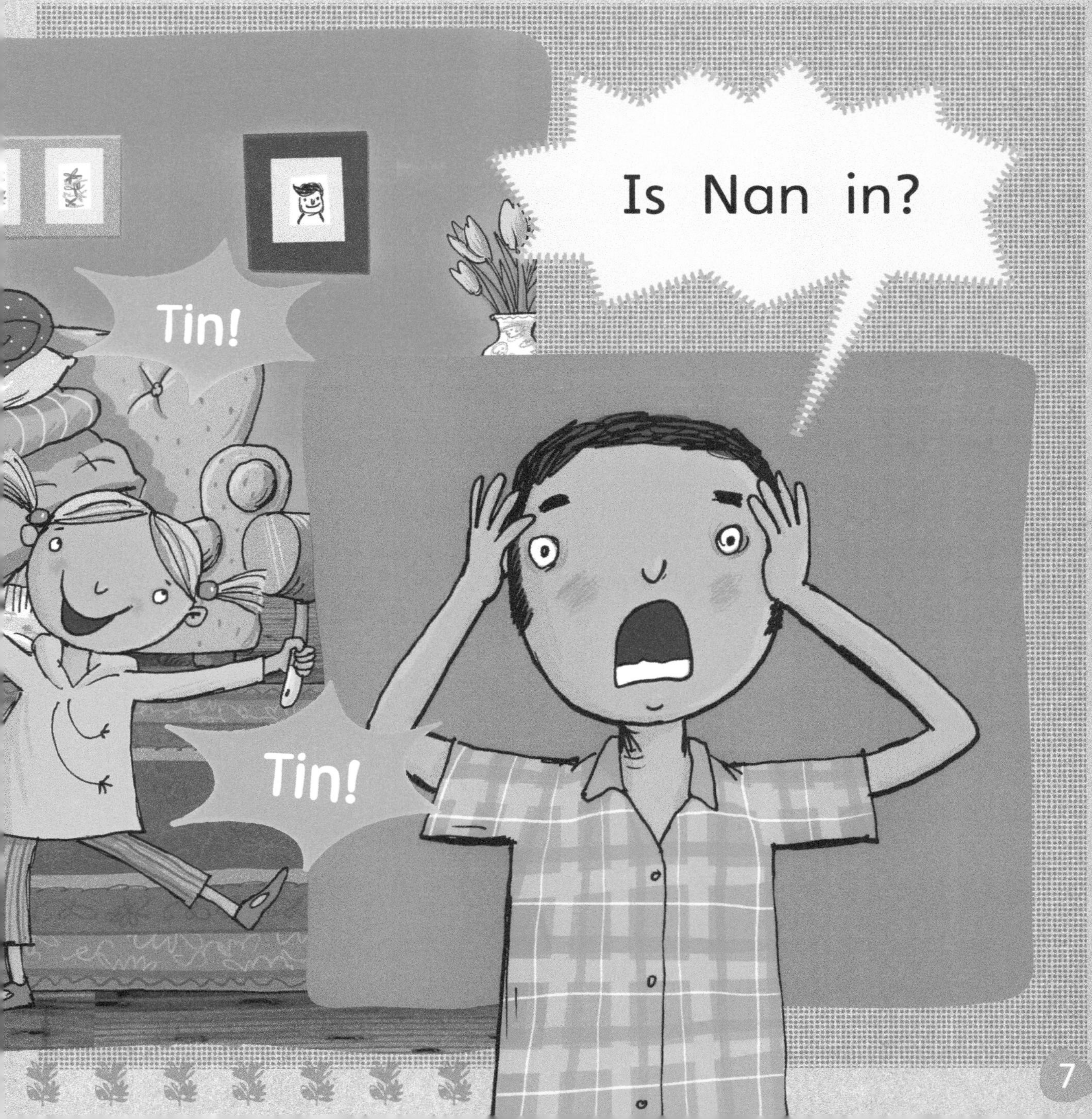
Tin!
Tin!
Is Nan in?

Nan is in!

It is a din!

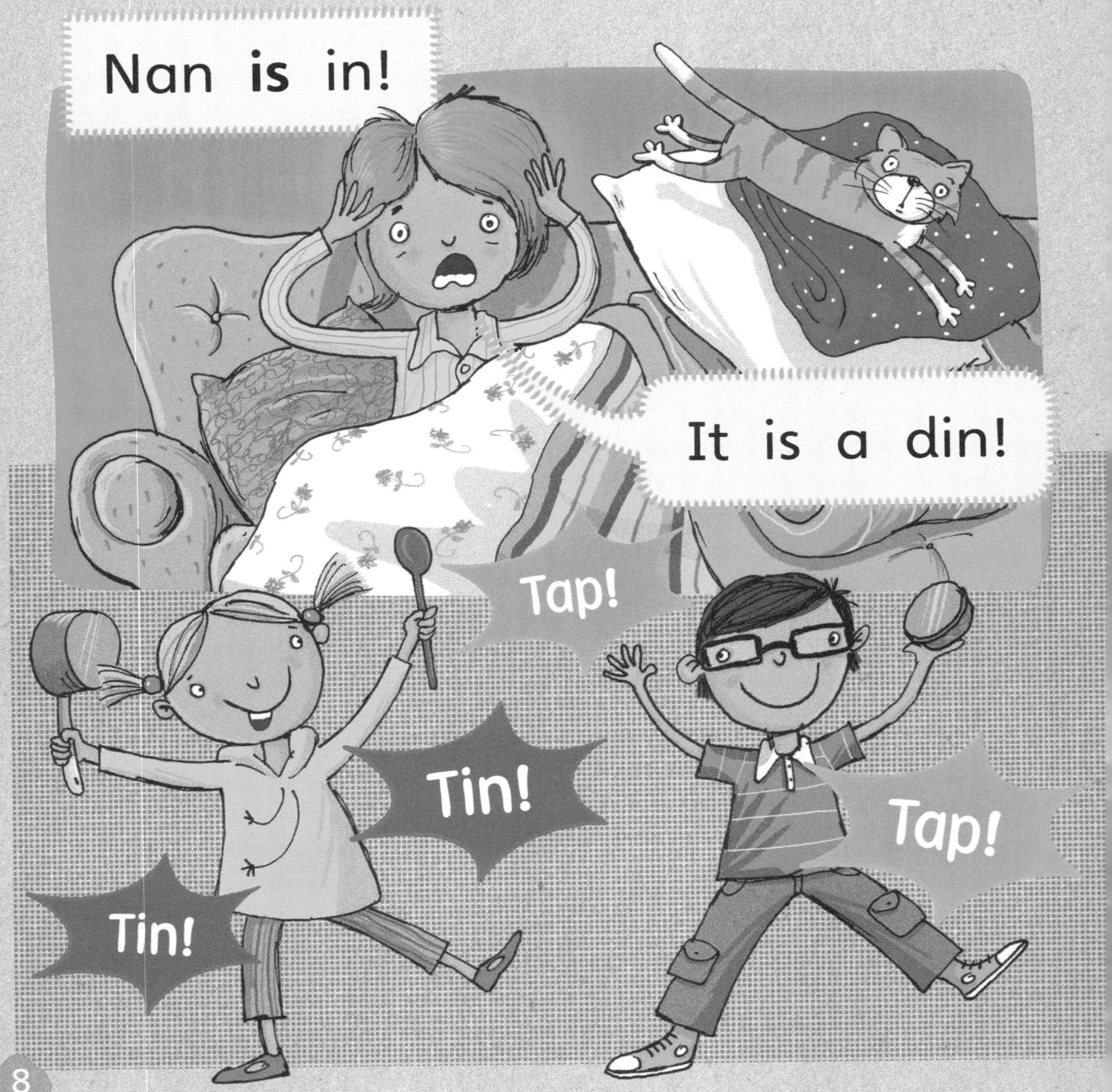